TRICK KNIFE THROWING CLASSICS

TRICK KNIFE THROWING CLASSICS

HOW TO THROW KNIVES
ELMER PUTTS

THE ART OF KNIFE THROWING
FRANK DEAN

COACHWHIP PUBLICATIONS

Greenville, Ohio

Trick Knife Throwing Classics
© 2014 Coachwhip Publications

How to Throw Knives, by Elmer Putts
Published 1935
The Art of Knife Throwing, by Frank Dean
First published 1937, second edition 1948
No claims made on public domain material.

ISBN 1-61646-276-0
ISBN-13 978-1-61646-276-5

Cover: Knife thrower by Lok Men Shi

CoachwhipBooks.com

Two classic booklets on knife throwing tricks are reprinted here for entertainment purposes only. Please note that some of these tricks are dangerous.

No. 1096

How to Throw Knives

By Elmer Putts

Introduction to Knives and Knife Throwing

In pre-historic times among the primitive tribes, the early weapons were made from stones and flint. These served as cutting tools for hunting game, for working materials and for defensive purposes. These stones were chipped and fashioned so as to provide a sharp edge. As the knowledge of metals became known, cutting tools were made of iron and bronze. The Romans taught the early Britons how to work iron which was the beginning of the famous English cutlery. The Norman invaders brought over many skilled metal workers. Gradually the bulk of the world's cutlery and famous weapons were developed in England, France and Germany.

It soon became evident that the real quality of the knife depended upon the steel that was in it. In the early days of the manufacture of cutlery, cast steel and shear steel was used. The manufacture of steel has since become an exacting science but during those times, high grade steel usually meant steel with a low carbon content. Even a small percentage of carbon causes steel to become brittle, so it was necessary to remove as much of this as possible to make steel for cutlery. Now most knives are made from stainless steel. After the knife is fashioned, it is hardened and tempered. Then it is ground to give it the best cutting edge.

With the development of firearms the importance and use of the knife has diminished, although in many places of the world it remains the sole weapon of defense. Even during modern warfare, a knife is still an essential part of the soldier's equipment.

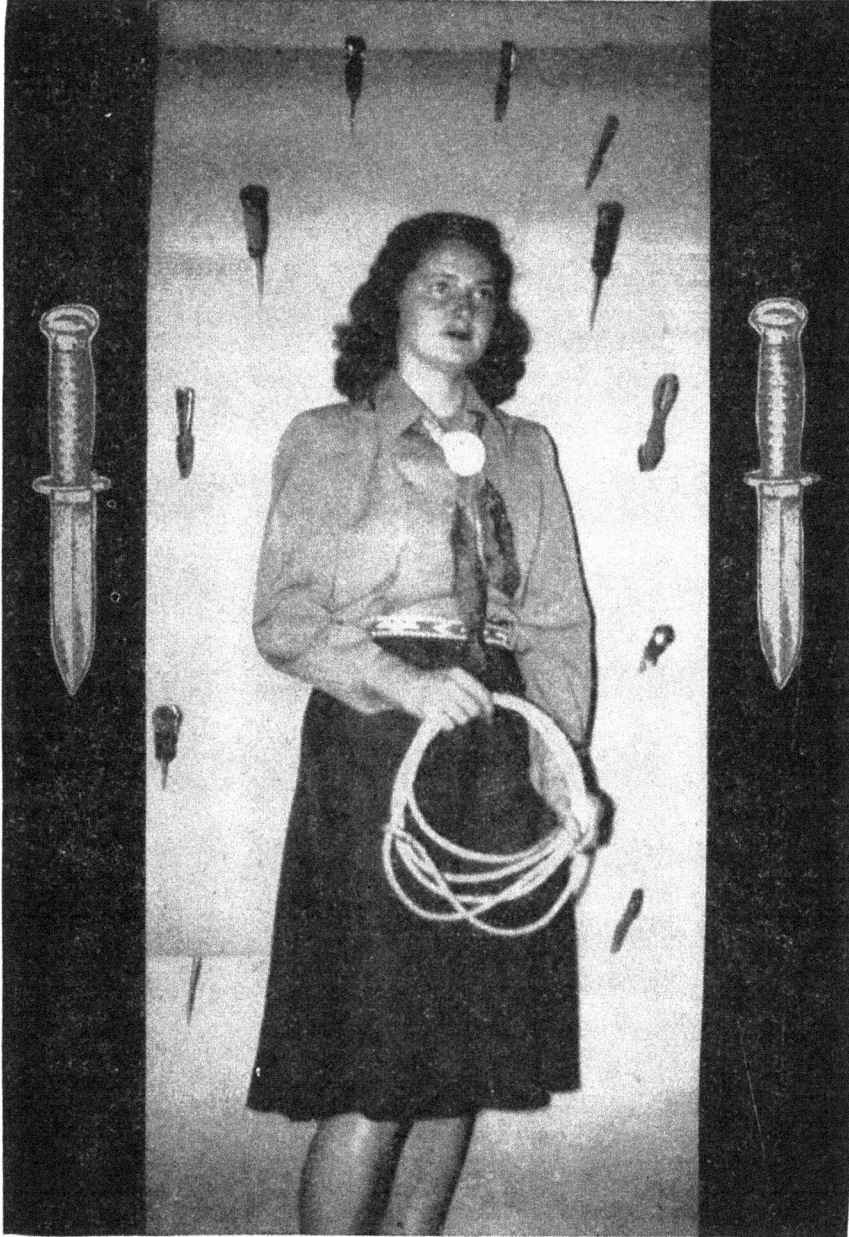

Elmer Putts, Author and Amateur Knife Thrower of Greenbush, Wisconsin, Tries His Skill Throwing Knives at Pretty Florence Smith.

The Proper Selection of a Throwing Knife

Almost any knife can be thrown and made to hit a target with some combination of luck and skill. However, the more luck that is required, the less control you have over the success of each throw. Until comparatively recently, no effort was made to design knives primarily for throwing, so the natural result was that there was no art of knife throwing that could be reduced to a science which would enable you to control the accuracy and hitting power of each throw. With the development of precision-made knives, knife throwing is less a matter of luck and more a matter of skill. These knives have been especially designed so that with only a little practice and experience, you can spot your target and make a hit with accuracy.

The development of balanced throwing knives was only one of two important reasons for successful **controlled knife throwing.** The second reason was the uniform method of throwing. Once you have perfected your own throwing method, stick to it---make it uniform and automatic so that each throw is exactly like the previous one. More will be explained to you about the throwing motion in a later chapter where standard methods now in use will be described and illustrated.

In the selection of a knife it is well to remember that it should embody these important features:

1. DURABLE FOR HARD USAGE.

2. BALANCED FOR SMOOTH TURNING.

3. DOUBLE EDGE POINT.

DURABLE FOR HARD USAGE. In order to make a knife penetrate a target when thrown from a distance, there has to be sufficient power behind it. The harder the material which the knife must pierce, the more power that will be required. For this reason, most throws will impose upon the knife hard and rough usage. This means that the knife itself must be ruggedly built to withstand this constant punishment. Folding pocket knives or jacknives very seldom satisfy this requirement. Kitchen and household knives are generally made of light weight steel that is flexible and not sufficiently rigid so that they vibrate and quiver when thrown. Even hunting knives are not usually built to stand persistent throwing.

The type of steel is very important. While for household purposes ordinary steel is usually sufficient, in a throwing knife the steel must be thoroughly tempered so that it is resilient. Thus it will not become brittle and break when in constant use. It is better to use a soft steel that will bend than a hard steel without sufficient temper.

The handles of ordinary knives are seldom designed for hard usage. They need not be fancy, but they must be durable. In the case of some throwing knives, the handle is just a continuation of the blade

Miscellaneous Hunting Knives

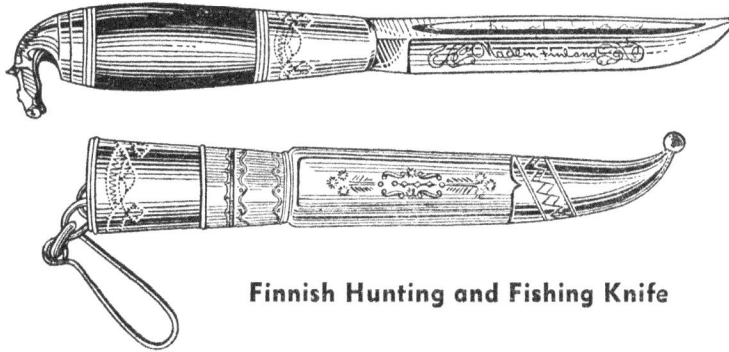

Finnish Hunting and Fishing Knife

These knives are not suitable for use as throwing knives

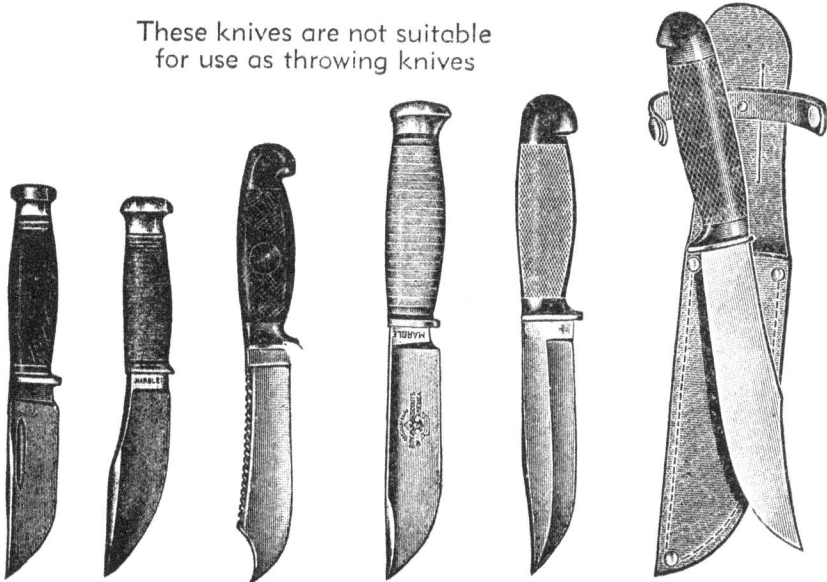

without any real grip for comfortable holding. Wooden and plastic handles have a tendency to break easily so it is best to use a knife with a leather or composition rubber handle. These will take plenty of abuse and last for a long time.

BALANCED FOR SMOOTH TURNING. The principle behind controlled throwing is to use a uniform motion and to know the "rate

Knifecrafter's Throwing Knife

Designed by a famous European Knife Throwing Expert for Knifecrafter's. Has weight lessened slotted handle with specially forged tapers. Expertly balanced for maximum penetration. 7¾-inches long, weight 8 ounces.

Knifecrafter's Throwing Knife

Light in weight, yet beautifully balanced and finished. Double bevel cutting blade shaped similar to a dagger with a point that penetrates easily and deeply. Electrically heat-treated high carbon tool steel. 7¾-inches, weight 8 ounces.

Hunting and Throwing Knife   →

This is the popular all-purpose design that serves as a comfortable hunting knife and a well-balanced double-edged throwing knife.

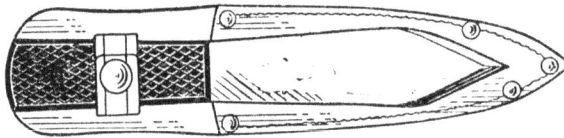

Famous European Throwing Knife

Europeans are famous for the high development of knife throwing and this is reflected in the expert design of these English throwing knives. Heavy, broad beam, keenly sharpened blades. Rubber composition handles. Fine Sheffield steel. Length 7-inches, weight 7 ounces

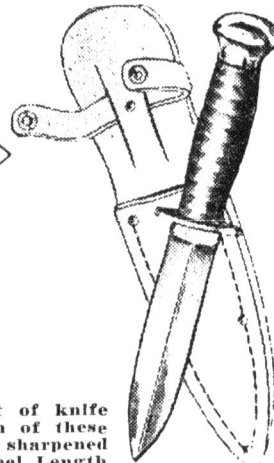

and distance of turn" for the knife you are using. This means that the knife must turn uniformly in the air and to do this, it must be properly balanced. It does not have to be perfectly balanced in the center, but it will be found that the closer the knife comes to a perfect balance, the easier it is to control. Most knives tend to be **"handle heavy"**. A heavy handle reduces the effectiveness of a knife unless you make a perfect hit (which does not occur very often) since it has a tendency to continue to turn the knife after it has made the hit. A knife that is **"blade heavy"** has a tendency to bury itself in the target even when a poor hit is made. This is a considerable advantage. If you decide to make or redesign a knife for throwing, it is a good idea to keep this in mind.

DOUBLE EDGE POINT. While not absolutely essential, it is very desirable to have a double edge knife. No knife manufactured primarily for throwing is made with a single sharp edge. The point must cut and penetrate like a spear so both edges should be sharp for maximum effectiveness.

While it is true that any knife which meets these requirements can be used for knife throwing, it is amazing how few ordinary knives do have all three characteristics. You will find many types of knives illustrated in this book which will serve as a helpful guide to those who desire to select a good throwing knife. Or, you can make your own knife from the instructions given in another chapter of this book.

Making Your Own Throwing Knife

There was a time when the only way to secure a good throwing knife was to make your own, but this is mostly a thing of the past. There are several good throwing knives on the market which make it easy for you to secure one. For that reason, little space is devoted to the making of your own knife.

Some people, for one reason or another, would prefer to make their own knife. If the proper tools are handy, it is not a really difficult job and you'll get a lot of satisfaction from knowing that you've got exactly the style of knife you want.

The illustration shown here will serve as a pattern for making your knife. The scale in this illustration is each square represents 1 inch so that the overall length of the knife illustrated is 10 inches.

This pattern can be used to make the following three styles of knife blades:

SABER BLADE. This is the style as illustrated.

DIAMOND BLADE. You will note that right down the middle of the knife from the point back through the middle of the handle a dotted line divides the knife in half. If the same pattern used in the upper half of the knife is also used in the lower half, you get a symmetrically patterned blade called a "diamond blade".

SWORD BLADE. If the bottom half of the pattern is used for both the upper and lower halves of the blade, you get the familiar "sword blade".

Actually it does not make a great deal of difference which style of blade you select. This knife is designed so that the great majority of the weight is located in the blade. It is important that the knife be about 10 inches long as this is an ideal size for target and stage work. It makes a durable knife.

Pattern of the knife should be cut out of 12 or 14 gauge sheet iron of good quality. It should be buffed smoothly for nice finish. This metal can usually be secured for practically no cost at a steel warehouse or at a foundry. Explain the use you are going to make of it so that you get highest quality steel. Stainless steel can be used for this purpose to good advantage.

How to Throw Knives

Once you have cut the steel to shape and finished it, you are ready to put the edge on the point. This can be done with a grinding wheel or file for the most part, with the final sharpening done with a finer stone. Be sure to put edges on both sides of the point and on both sides of the steel so that blade is balanced. If knife is to be used only for throwing, the edges need not extend very far back towards the handle. An inch or two will be sufficient.

For the handle, you are left pretty much to decide for yourself what you desire to use. Boot sole leather about 3/8-inch thick is very good. It will wear well and is comfortable. Composition rubber is also good. For those who want something a little fancy, pearl or imitation pearl plastic looks very well. These are especially good for stage work. The handles should be attached with solid rivets at least 1/8-inch in diameter. Smooth out the handle by filing or buffing it into a comfortable shape

This outline tells you the general method and pattern for your something more elaborate. These can be made as ornamental as you thing more elaborate. These can be made as ornamental as you desire both in shape and decoration. Even a fancy throwing knife need not be very expensive, yet it will add quite a bit to the showmanship of your throwing.

Pattern for Throwing Knife

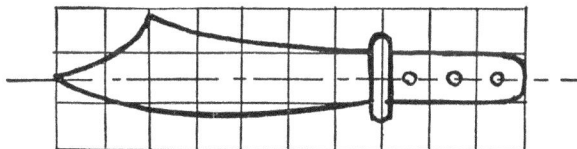

Each square represents 1 inch. Overall length of knife is 10 inches. Three styles can be made from above pattern. SABER BLADE by using entire pattern as illustrated; DIAMOND BLADE by using upper half design for both upper and lower outline of blade; SWORD BLADE by using the lower half design. Variations in handle and blade design can be made for those who want an ornamental knife to add showmanship to their throwing.

How to Throw a Knife

The elements which go to make up an accurate throw are remarkably simple, yet they must be done with precision to secure the uniform results which are the basis for controlled throwing.

With just a little patient practice, you will find that your throws hit the target "point first" with remarkable regularity. You will experience a real thrill as you discover that at last you are actually the master of the throw and that you can place the knife where you want it. When you first get this thrill, remember that you have just begun to enjoy controlled knife throwing and that from this simple beginning, all sorts of fascinating variations and stunts can be developed.

Knife throwing is growing in popularity, but it is still uncommon enough to enable you to be among the first to excite your friends with a few simple tricks. As you learn more and more stunts, you will find that your hobby has developed into a profitable source of added income if you desire to exploit your talents at sportsmen's shows, carnivals, exhibitions, on the stage or in any of a number of other ways.

But now to explain the proper method of throwing. There are just two essential parts to the throw and they are (1) the way you grip the knife; and, (2) the arm motion. All trick throws are a variation of the forward throw. Once you have mastered it, try to get the "feel" of the throw so that you get the feeling that you can make the knife do just about anything you want it to do. When you get that feeling, make your own variations with more assurance that you understand what you are doing. While the throwing motion is a fixed pattern, do not try to make it entirely automatic, but try to feel that you are controlling the flight and power of the knife right to the target.

The Grip

There are three methods for holding the knife. The most popular method is to grip the blade in either of the two positions illustrated. The other method is to grip the handle. It is well to learn to throw a knife with any of these three grips, but for the beginner, the blade grip is easier to control.

Generally speaking, if the knife is well balanced, use the blade

The Grip

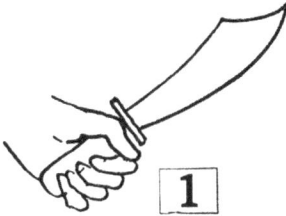

1

Handle Grip

Used by some stage performers, but especially handy for use by sportsmen with ordinary hunting knives. Knife is held the same way it is gripped for hand work.

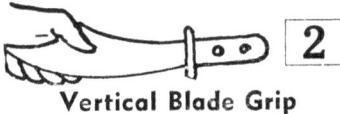

2

Vertical Blade Grip

Knife is held with blade vertical. Comfortable grip for a smooth throw. Imparts a greater spin to knife and is ideal for short throws.

Horizontal Blade Grip

The grip used by European knife throwing experts for greatest control. Cannot pivot between fingers. Weight of knife rests in hand giving you better "feel". Produces a slow turning throw which gives better chance for good hit and deep penetration. We recommend this grip where no cutting is required and knife must only pierce target.

3

grip. If it is "handle heavy" use the handle grip, and if it is "blade heavy" use the blade grip. In this way, the main weight will be in your hand when you are going through the throwing motion and it will be easier to control.

HANDLE GRIP. Illustration 1 shows the handle grip. This is useful for sportsmen who normally carry hunting knives in their hands. Since this is the natural grip, the knife is ready for use eiether as a hand or throwing knife. Also used when knife is "handle heavy". Some stage performers prefer this grip, though it is not as popular as the blade grip.

VERTICAL BLADE GRIP. Illustration 2 shows the vertical blade grip. The blade of the knife is held in a vertical position. Its main disadvantage is that the knife has a tendency to pivot in the hand before it is released when throwing, thus giving it an additional spin that destroys the accuracy and control of the throw. It will be found that this grip is absolutely necessary for many stunt throws including cutting effects.

HORIZONTAL BLADE GRIP. Illustration 3 shows the horizontal or flat blade grip, in an upraised position. We recommend this grip when you are throwing at a target, since it offers more control than any other grip. There is almost no chance for the knife to pivot in the hand and if you are careful to keep your wrist rigid, the only motion imparted to the knife comes from the arm. In this way you will quickly learn to make controlled throws. When this grip is used, the knife turns much more slowly in flight. The chances for a hit are better since the knife turns so slowly that it will travel one or two feet with the point forward. While this is the best grip for ordinary target throwing, it cannot be used for cutting and other stunts since the cutting edge of blade is flat.

While it is good for the beginner to know the different grips so that he may vary his throwing as he progresses, it will be wise for you to use one grip until you have mastered it, then introduce your own variations. We suggest either of the blade grips, whichever seems to give you the most comfortable feeling.

Interesting Information on Knives and Knife Throwing

A certain veriety of slang names have been used in connection with knives that might interest you. It is sometimes called a **slasher, stabber, pin, ripper, cold steel, toad stabber, Arkansas toothpick, Kansas neck blister, armstrong mower; a pocket knife is known as a dagger, dirk, pigsticker, prat cutter, toad stabber, man and wife.** A knife throwing act at a carnival is known as a suicide squadron or a hooligan (Wild West show).

Knife throwing acts are used both in the movies and in side shows. The movies pay extremely good money for small bit parts to good knife throwers.

A useful idea when practicing knife throwing is to attach a light, but sturdy string to it. This should be connected to some part of handle. If light string is used, it will not affect the throwing characteristics to any great extent, but it does make it easy to retrieve the knife. String can be up to about 20 feet long without seriously affecting your accuracy. Keep the cord slack so that it will be given out quickly. This stunt is also useful when throwing knife up into a tree or inaccessible place. A few jerks of the string will usually bring the knife back home.

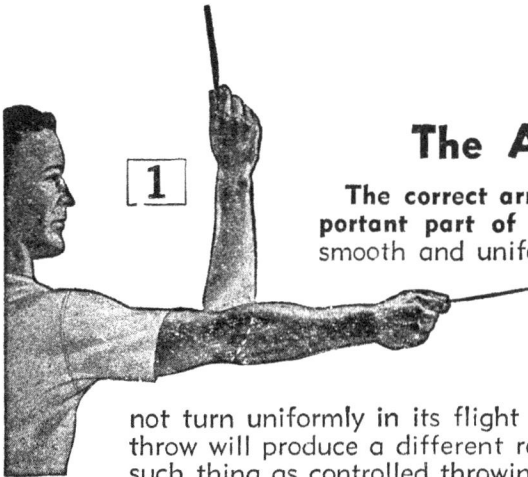

The Arm Motion

The correct arm motion is the most important part of the throw. It should be smooth and uniform. It is important that **no wrist action or flip accompany the throw.** Any wrist action will give the knife an additional spin so that it will not turn uniformly in its flight to the target. Thus each throw will produce a different result and there will be no such thing as controlled throwing.

For short throws sufficient power can be secured from using just the forearm (see illustration 1). For long throws or for harder hits, the entire arm is used (see illustration 2). The principle is the same in both cases, the only difference being in the amount of effort behind each throw and the point of the pivot. In one case the pivot is at the elbow, and in the other the pivot is at the shoulder.

THERE IS NO WRIST ACTION. The knife is gripped lightly but firmly. The arm is extended fully so that it forms a straight line with the knife. It is at this point that you take your aim at the target. Then slowly bring the arm to an upright position, keeping your eye on the target. You are now ready for the throwing motion.

Start the throw by a smooth forward action of the upraised arm, allowing it to pass through the horizontal position with a full follow through. You release the knife just before the arm becomes horizontal, so that knife actually flies out in almost a direct line for the target. Do not grip knife too tightly. There is no wrist action or flip to the action, the knife is released from the hand and flies to the target. **Be sure to relax.**

Any additional movement of the wrist or fingers affects the rate of turn. While this is a simple action, until the beginner gains complete mastery of the arm movement, satisfactory results will not be obtained.

Once you have experimented with arm movement, you are ready to determine the **RATE OF TURN** of the knife you are using. Look at illustration 3. This illustration shows how the knife turns in the air before hitting target. It will be seen that if you are using the blade grip, the knife must make at least a ½ turn for knife to penetrate target (starting from position D). Or, it could be thrown from position B so that it describes 1 ½ turns before hitting target. It will be seen that once you have determined the **RATE OF TURN** you will know exactly where you must stand in order to hit the target.

This **RATE OF TURN** is determined by experiment, but with a few practice throws and carefully watching the results, you can figure this out rather quickly.

Stand about 5 feet from the target. At this distance, the knife when thrown with a blade point grip should not make more than half a turn. By moving backwards or forwards you can find the position where it describes a half turn and then hits target squarely. When you have determined this position, you will be throwing from position D (see illustration) which represents one-half turn. Now measure the distance **FROM THE OUTSTRETCHED HAND to the target.** This represents half a turn. By doubling it, you can get the distance required for one full turn.

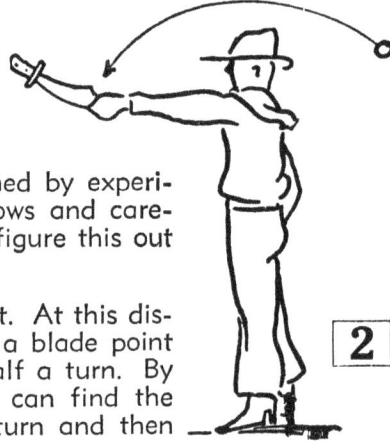

Let us say that you have found the closest distance to the target that knife will penetrate it. Suppose that distance from OUT-STRETCHED HAND TO TARGET is 3 feet. This represents half of a complete turn. For a full turn, the knife would require 6 feet. If you wish to throw the knife so that it describes 1 ½ turns before striking target, it will be necessary to stand 6 plus 3 plus the length of outstretched arm (say 2 feet) which would make 11 feet from target. If you wish to stand further from target, you can increase this distance by any multiple of 6 feet such as 6, 12, 18, 24, 36, etc.

In the same manner you can figure how far away to stand for a handle throw, except that a handle throw must go through a full turn before it strikes target. Thus from position C, the thrower would be 6 feet plus 2 feet (length of outstretched arm) or 8 feet from target. He could also make the throw from 8 plus 6, or 14 feet; or, 14 plus 6, or 20 feet, etc. If you will study the illustration it will become apparent how you can calculate the exact distance once you have determined the rate of turn.

How to Throw Knives

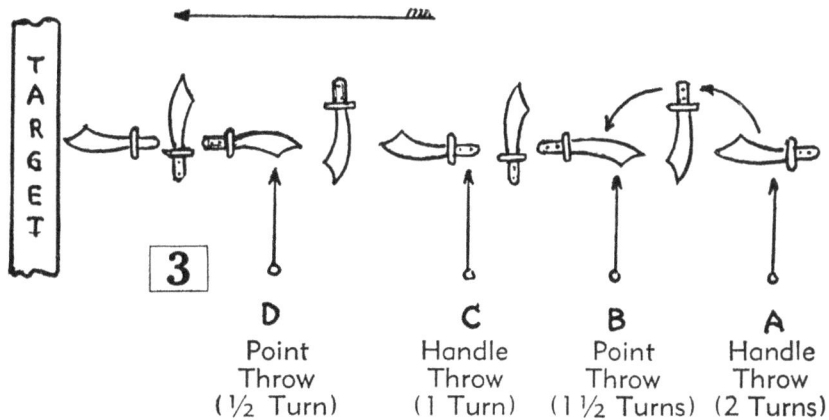

D	C	B	A
Point Throw (½ Turn)	Handle Throw (1 Turn)	Point Throw (1½ Turns)	Handle Throw (2 Turns)

How to Determine Correct Throwing Distance

1. Stand as close to target as possible so that knife will describe one-half turn (so that it leaves hand from position D). If you are just beginning, stand 5 feet from target and move nearer or farther away until knife hits target squarely.

2. Subtract length of your arm from distance to target and this will give the distance knife requires for one-half turn. (Thus, if your arm is 2 feet long and knife hits squarely with one-half turn standing 5 feet from target, distance required for half turn is 3 feet; for full turn, 6 feet).

3. Once you have determined RATE OF TURN you will know exactly where to stand for either handle or point throw. (If rate of turn is 6 feet and you wish to make a handle throw, you can stand either 8 feet (6 feet for full turn plus 2 feet for arm length) from target or 14 feet from target (12 feet for two full turns plus 2 feet for arm length) from target, etc.)

Trick Knife Throwing

By now, if you have carefully followed the instructions, you are fairly adept at throwing a knife at a target and hitting it with reasonable accuracy. Up until now, we have considered only a stationary target directly in front of the thrower. This, of course, is the easiest type of target to hit. For practice, it would be a good idea to move the target around---up high and down low---practicing your throws until you can hit the bull's eye no matter where the target might be located.

Trick throws require considerable practice in order to perfect them, yet they offer considerable satisfaction and amusement both for your friends as well as yourself. Good knife throwers are rare. The team of Frank and Bernice Dean were well known around the world for their act. Al Barnes, Frank Chicarello and Bennie Pete were three others whose knife throwing artistry thrilled millions.

A movie filmed by Metro Goldwyn Mayer called for a duel between two knife throwers. Each knife thrower was equipped with a small wooden target or shield. As a girl danced between them, each one had to throw his knives past the girl's head and into the target. Jack Cavanaugh and Frank Dean were the two knife throwers used and they displayed remarkable knife throwing ability. A slight miscalculation might have been fatal!

You will be amazed at the amount of control you can exercise over the knives if you are willing to really practice. There are several good stunts described in this chapter and it will be wise for you to select one or two and practice them until you have mastered them before going on to another one. Before you start any kind of trick throwing, especially if you are giving a performance, it is best to warm up to the harder stunts by doing a series of simple throws first to get the feel back.

Moving Targets

Hitting a moving target is something every good knife thrower must learn sooner or later and the sooner you learn it, the better off you will be. It gives you a complete new mastery over the knives and more confidence in your ability. No longer are you following a fixed throwing pattern, but you have to use judgment.

How to Throw Knives

First make up a target of soft pine wood about 2 inches thick and one foot in diameter. Practice throwing at this target for a while. Then mount it on a string about 3 feet long and surpend it so that it will swing like a pendulum. Set the target in motion and practice your throws at this moving target.

As you improve to a point where you are almost 100% perfect, you can add variations to this such as reducing size of target or have someone hold target by string from arm's length.

Bennie Pete would strap a small target to an assistant's chest or back and throw knives into it at a distance of 12 feet. We don't recommend this for you since one slip would mean the end of the act, but it shows what a really expert knife thrower can do.

Throwing Two Knives at a Time

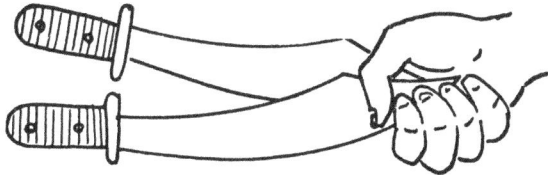

This is not a difficult thing to do since both knives are gripped together and thrown together as you would throw one knife. While more than two knives can be thrown at one time, the number thrown being limited by the size of the knives and the size of your hand, but any number more than two will prove hard to control. With a little practice you will find that you can control the spread between the knives as they hit the target.

You can use either the horizontal or the vertical blade throw, depending on how you want the knives to separate.

Cross Knives

A good stunt that will test your skill at knife throwing. The idea of this is to throw two knives, one right after the other, so they make a cross after hitting the target.

For a vertical cross, one knife must be thrown a little closer than the regular distance so that it will slant with handle hanging slightly downward; second knife must be thrown a little farther than regular distance so that knife will slant with handle upward when it hits target. If both throws have been accurate, the knives will form a cross.

How to Throw Knives

For a horizontal cross, knives must be thrown from one side, then the other side. Knives are thrown from either a little closer or a little farther than regular distance so that knife strikes at an angle instead of head-on. Some performers throw one knife from each hand at the same time to produce the horizontal effect.

This is a good stunt to do, but requires plenty of practice.

Overhand Throw While Lying on Back

This throw looks a lot more difficult than it actually is. Shoulder should rest approximately at the same spot as you would stand in a regular throw. Use the same overhand motion we have illustrated.

Backward Throw

This can be done in a variety of ways depending upon the performer. You can throw it blind as shown in our illustration, or you can look over your shoulder, under the arm, use a mirror, etc. Essentially they are all the same throw and depend upon the performer getting in the right position. Performer stands regular distance from target.

Actually you will find this a difficult throw to control and will require much practice. An entire new set of muscles are used that are not familiar with the routine action you have practiced.

Throwing Knife from Between the Legs

This is very similar to the backward throw with the exception that the motion goes between the legs instead of to one side. The performer can watch the target as he makes his throw which aids the accuracy of the throw.

A little experimenting will be necessary to find the correct throwing distance as generally it will be found to be a few inches closer than the regular distance.

The Lifted Leg Throw

This is a stunt used by Benny Pete and one that is difficult to do with accuracy. The effect is to walk along parallel to the target and as you take a step with your right foot your right hand makes an underhand throw under the leg. (If you are right handed). This is a very effective trick and looks very good on the stage.

Throwing From Other Positions

As you will probably have gathered by now, there is almost no limit to the number of positions from which you can throw knives---even standing on your head. Each performer works up a little act of his own, introducing a new throwing position, but essentially they are all pretty much the same. Once you have run through these here, you have pretty well mastered the fundamental throws and you can proceed to vary them to suit your own idea of showmanship.

Some add other novelties to their act such as rifle shooting, rope spinning, juggling, etc., to make the stunts look harder. After all, in most knife throwing acts you do have one free hand that you can put to work! Comedy stunts can be worked out, too.

The Master Knife Throwing Stunt---Outlining a Person

Perhaps the climax of every knife throwing act is when the performer undertakes to have an assistant stand before a large target and then proceeds to outline the assistant with a number of knives. This requires a thorough knowledge and ability of knife throwing together with a cool head and steady nerves.

The assistant can assume any position. Perhaps the easiest method is for the assistant to stand straight, facing either sideways or outwards. In either case the performer can throw knives up and down each side in a vertical row.

The variations from this fundamental position are many, the illustration giving you one idea. To add to the stunt you can place balloons around the assistant as targets, breaking each balloon with a throw.

Outlining a Person Completely Hidden

There are a few knife throwers in the country who are doing a very spectacular and risky stunt that should prove a real challenge to the skill of even the best knife throwers. It would be foolish to underestimate the amount of skill required to throw knives at an unseen human target, since even among the professional knife throwers, deep wounds have been received through carelessness.

Without trying to minimize its dangers, however, the stunt is somewhat simpler than it first appears. In this stunt the assistant stands in front of a target and is covered with either newspapers, a large sheet of paper, or some such screen. The assistant is entirely covered with the exception of the feet.

The feet supply the performer with the only guide for making his throws. Most performers prefer to work up one side, starting from the bottom since the foot provides a pretty good guide at this point.

If you follow a fixed routine in your knife throwing the assistant behind the screen will know exactly which knife is coming next. In this way he can shift his weight from one foot to the other and bend his body (without moving his feet) to allow as much as eight or ten inches added protection from the target. If your act is well rehearsed the shifting of this weight is not noticed by the audience and gives a good knife thrower the added margin required, especially around the head.

When the last knife is thrown, the assistant breaks out of the center of the target, leaving the paper and knives ready for inspection by the audience so that there can be no charge of skullduggery. It is wise to point out that the feet are in full sight of the audience at all times so that the audience will know that the assistant is always there.

Cutting Stunts With Throwing Knives

Most cutting stunts are really very easy and merely require a little practice. Almost all of them use the straight-forward throw which you should have perfected by this time. Of course, many variations can be made to make these tricks more difficult, but we prefer to outline them in their simplest form and if you wish to combine a string cutting effect with a backward throw or throwing while standing on your head, good luck to you!

All cutting stunts are made using either the vertical blade grip or the handle grip with blade vertical.

You will notice when reading this chapter that we refer a great deal to the rate of turn of the knife. It is important that you understand exactly what this means for all knife throwing is based upon it. If you have become hazy, refer back to the illustration which shows the knife turning through the air. THE RATE OF TURN IS THE DISTANCE THE KNIFE TRAVELS IN THE AIR IN ORDER TO MAKE ONE COMPLETE REVOLUTION.

You will understand the importance of this when we tell you that you must know the position of the cutting edge of the knife blade as it travels through the air so that it cuts the string, paper, flowers, etc. See the illustration.

Paper Cutting

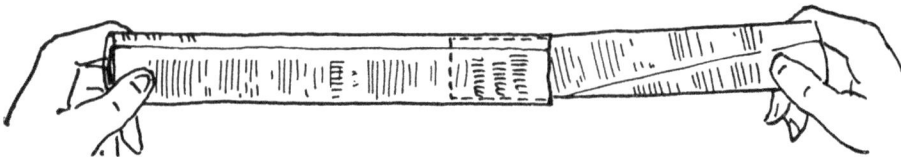

This is a good stunt to begin with since there is a trick to it that makes it very easy. The effect: a strip of paper is held in front of a target. The performer throws a knife at the target apparently during which the knife blade apparently cuts the paper then sticks into the target.

The secret is in the paper. Get a strip of paper about three feet long and about four inches wide. Fold each piece of paper over lengthwise and glue so that it forms a flat tube. Telescope the end of one tube into the end of the other tube about three inches. From a distance, this will not be noticed, but when the knife is flying through the air, it is only necessary for some part of the knife to hit the paper and it will cause the two sections to come apart as if cut! Of course you have to be a good enough knife thrower to hit the paper!

Paper should be held one-fourth of the distance knife requires in air to make one complete turn. If rate of turn is 8 feet, then paper should be held 2 feet from target. Thus knife blade will be in vertical position when it hits paper. Thus any part of knife will cause it to break.

Those who want to make this a legitimate trick can do so by just using a regular piece of paper and doing the trick as described.

String Cutting

This trick is done in a similar way to the paper cutting stunt, only it is not faked. Actually, if you are an accurate thrower, it is pretty easy. The string can be held in either of the two positions illustrated. As the knife travels through the air, the cutting blade neatly severs the string and continues on into the target.

The important thing to remember is how far from the target to hold the string. This distance should be equal to one fourth of the rate of turn. If the rate of turn for your knife and throw is one complete end over end turn in 8 feet, then you will hold the string one-fourth of the distance (or two feet) from the target. From the illustration in the chapter on knife throwing, it will be seen that knife blade is in a vertical cutting position, and will sever string, paper, etc., quite easily while in flight.

String should be held taut. Use black or colored string for better visibility for yourself and your audience. At least 14 or 15 inches of string should be held to give you an ample target. When throwing at string held overhead, throw to one side of head to minimize danger of an accident.

Cutting a Moving String

If you wish you can have two persons hold the string and move it up and down thus apparently making a more difficult target. However, if you have them limit the movement to the length of the cutting edge of the knife, you will see that it is not much more difficult than cutting a stationery string.

Cutting Flowers

This makes quite an effective stage presentation since the colorful flowers add in a considerable measure to the effect. A flower with a long stem should be used. The flower is held very much as you would hold a piece of string---one-quarter of a turn in front of the target. For best results, flowers with easily cut, yet rigid stems should be used. Ideal flowers to use are dandelions, dahlias, marigolds, poppies, tulips, geraniums, narcissus, etc. Flowers such as roses have heavy, tough stems which are not easily cut.

Exploding Balloons

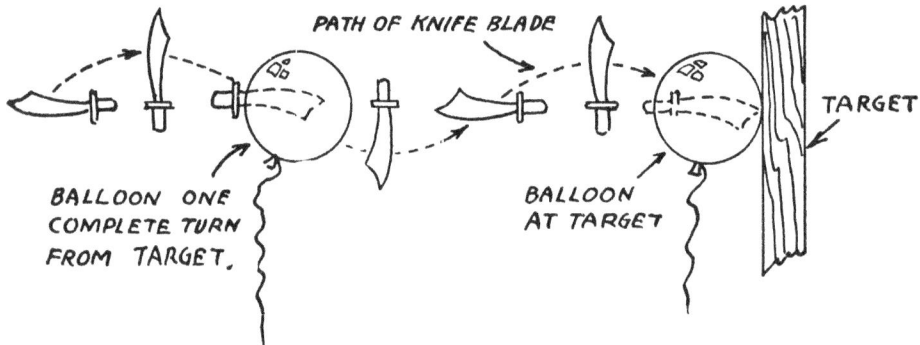

PATH OF KNIFE BLADE

TARGET

BALLOON ONE COMPLETE TURN FROM TARGET.

BALLOON AT TARGET

This is a popular stunt especially for children, though it is quite easy to do. You'll enjoy doing it and it makes good target practice. There is a great variety of ways this can be done and it will be limited only by your own ingenuity.

The simplest method is to put one or more balloons on your target board and then pick them off one after the other. Any bull's eye will explode the balloon so that knife sticks into the target. From the illustration of the knife in flight, you will remember that the knife blade comes round and down into target with cutting edge first. This will pierce and explode balloon.

A variation of this is to set up a balloon the distance equal to the rate of turn (one complete turn of knife) from the target. Then knife will pierce and explode balloon in mid-air and continue on to the target. You can have second balloon on target for double explosion. One performer could explode two and three balloons in mid-air before hitting the target balloon! Quite a feat that takes a powerful, accurate throw.

Halving a Swinging or Stationary Apple

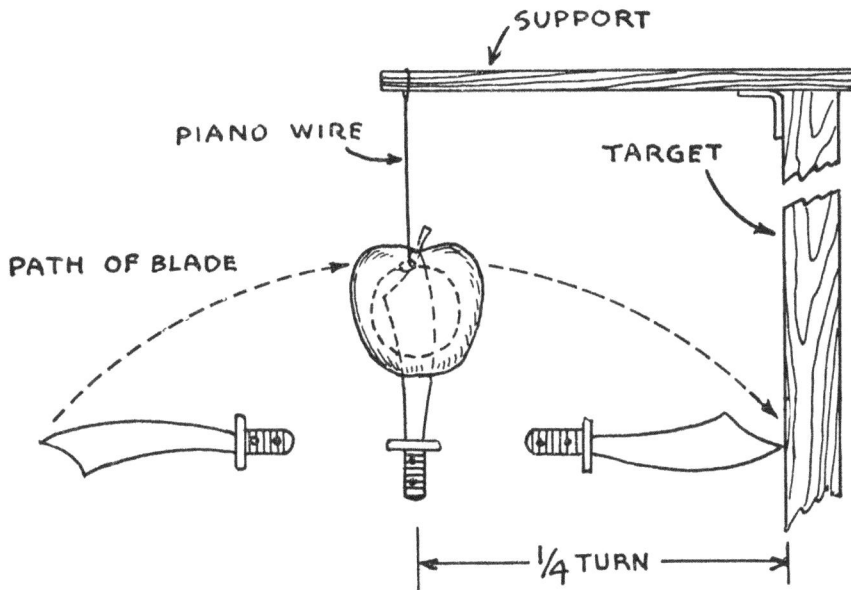

Quite an effective trick which is easy to do on a stationary apple and requires practice to do on a swinging apple. It is very popular with audiences so you will want to master it and add it to your program.

The apple is mounted on a wire in the form of a pendulum in front of the target. The apple must be the same distance from the target equal to the distance required for one-quarter of a complete turn. This is the same distance you use in paper, string and flower cutting effects. The knife blade hits the apple when it is in a vertical position.

How to Throw Knives

Use light steel wire (piano wire) to suspend the apple from support. If pendulum is about 30 inches long, it will oscillate very well when you wish to hit the moving apple target.

To attach apple to wire, form a noose in the wire and slip apple into it. Pull wire taut until it breaks the skin and even cuts the apple about one-half inch or more. This will make the apple easier to sever and the wire also serves as a guide to the knife blade to make a cleaner, more nearly equal cut if the blade should hit the wire. Apple must be suspended so that noose is parallel to the flight of the knife.

This can be done either with the aid of a support as mentioned above or by having an assistant or spectator holding the wire from an outstretched hand.

Cutting Apple Sitting on Assistant's Head

This is also referred to as the "William Tell Stunt" since it requires hitting an apple while it is perched on top of the head of an assistant.

This is done exactly like the regular apple stunt except **KNIFE IS THROWN WITH A SIDE ARM MOTION, HORIZONTALLY, INSTEAD OF VERTICALLY.** The reason for this will be obvious. The knife blade must cut horizontally instead of vertically. If done vertically the knife handle would hit assistant and it would also be necessary to cut apple right down to the head which would be too close even for the most expert knife thrower! The horizontal throw will require practice, but even the best knife throwers hesitate before doing this stunt, so don't be too anxious to try this.

Professional knife throwers set the apple on assistant's hat. The hat is usually lined with metal to protect him in case of a miss. As a further safeguard, they throw knife from shortest possible distance so that better control is secured. To make it look further, however, you can step back one or two paces and step forward as you wind up for the throw. When throw is finished, take one or two backward steps---the audience will have their eyes on the apple.

This is a sensational stunt when performed to perfection, but one that is done only by the very best knief throwers. If you are not yet in that class---DO NOT TRY IT. One of the country's best known knife throwers did this trick for the movies and on the stage, but would never do it without constant daily practice.

Flaming Knives

The use of flaming knives is one of those stunts that is very spectacular to the audience yet extremely easy to perform. Of course, as with any knife throwing trick, you can make it more difficult by using trick throws, but an audience seldom appreciates these finer points. The sight of the flaming knife captures their attention. It is a good idea to focus the audience's attention on just one thing at a time, and in this way you can spread out your act to a greater extent.

Flaming knives require handles which will not burn (strangely enough) since the handle is dipped in kerosene or some other inflammable liquid. The knives are always thrown by the blade grip. Only the handle of the knife is flaming.

Another manner in which these knives can be used is to throw a series of treated, but unlighted, knives at a target. The last knife will be a flaming knife and is thrown below the others. This immediately sets the entire group aflame in one terrifying finish. The knives will flare up on each side of him and he can step quickly out without injury.

Other stunts will occur to you such as throwing a flaming knife at a hoop dipped in the kerosene. The entire hoop flames up. In a similar way other things can be made to ignite by the flaming knife. One performer had an ingenious stunt whereby he imbedded small pieces of flint in the target. When the knife struck the flint, the sparks ignited the knife. It was very mysterious to the audience. Use your imagination and devise your own new stunts.

Do not use flaming knives indoors except where building is absolutely fireproof.

Throwing Axe, Hatchet or Tomahawk

Some people are never satisfied---when they have mastered knife throwing, they want to throw axes and hatchets. Well, you'll find that the principles of good knife throwing may be applied in a general way to throwing heavier articles from axes to 14 inch spikes.

Axes, hatchets and tomahawks are all thrown using a handle grip. Lighter axes, cleavers (like those used by butchers) and tomahawks are thrown with an overhand throw; heavier axes are thrown with an underhand throw.

If you are using the ordinary sportsmen's hand hatchet or axe, you will find that it is necessary to stand about 14 feet from target. It may be necessary to move back or forward a short distance depending upon the size and weight of the axe, but this distance should pro-

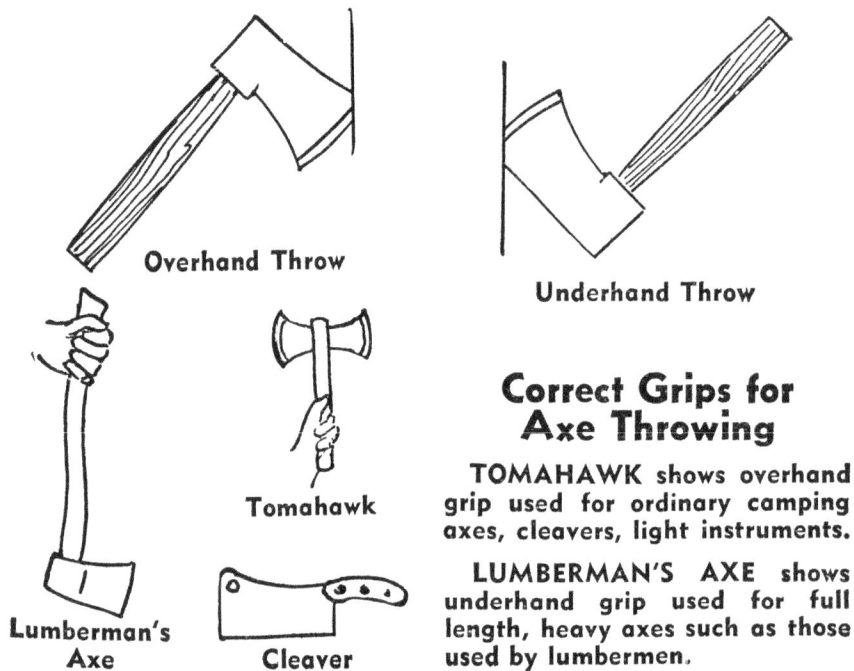

Overhand Throw

Underhand Throw

Tomahawk

Lumberman's Axe

Cleaver

Correct Grips for Axe Throwing

TOMAHAWK shows overhand grip used for ordinary camping axes, cleavers, light instruments.

LUMBERMAN'S AXE shows underhand grip used for full length, heavy axes such as those used by lumbermen.

vide you with a good point to experiment from. The longer the handle and the larger the axe the farther away from the target you will have to stand. For a full sized lumberman's axe, you should stand about 35 feet from target. When throwing a large axe of this sort, it is necessary to throw underhand. The underhand swing gives you more power with less effort; it reduces the risk of handling such a heavy cutting instrument.

Fancy Knives

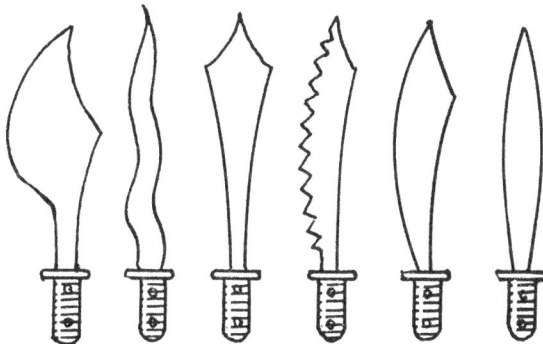

For some acts, knives of different shapes can be used. While there will be nothing different about their throwing characteristics, it looks more spectacular to the audience who think each one takes a different technique. Illustration shows just a few different styles, but you can have them made in weird shapes to your own desires.

When practicing, be sure to use a suitable target. Remember, the sharpest and most durable knife can take only so much abuse. A good target will make your knife last longer and keep it sharp. A bale of hay or straw makes a nice target if you don't hit the baling wire.

Knife Fighting

Deep within every person who learns to handle a knife is the desire to know how to use it for fighting in case of an emergency. Along with this is the desire to use it for hunting small game. Yes, the knife is a valuable weapon for every sportsman both for self-defense and for killing game, but **knife throwing** has its limitations.

Every reader of detective and adventure stories sooner or later comes in contact with the "deadly knife thrower" whose unerring accuracy is always fatal! In real life, however, knife throwers of this caliber are rare, though for short distances up to about thirty or forty feet, a well trained knife thrower can do considerable damage. For wild game hunting, the animal does not usually allow you to come within this short range.

Natives in countries where firearms have not been so highly developed seem to have developed a proficiency for knife throwing that in many cases is remarkable.

For knife fighting, it is necessary to learn an entirely new type of throw. This is called a POINT FORWARD THROW. As we have seen, in all the throws we have learned so far, the knife turns in the air, so that only for a short time is the blade traveling point forward--- the position in which it will be most effective. The reason this method of throw is used is for better control. Just as the rifling in a gun barrel rotates the bullet before it leaves the gun for greater accuracy, so does the rotating of the knife make it describe a more uniform path through the air. Then, too, a knife that is thrown through the air as described for target work can be thrown consistently the same, the only variation being in the amount of effort behind the throw. Even the amount of power behind the throw has little effect upon the accuracy, but merely gives the knife more sock when it hits the target.

For knife fighting, it must be thrown so that it travels with blade first throughout its flight, so that no matter what the distance, no matter how much the target moves forward or away from you, when the knife strikes, the point is there to meet the target. We will now explain several ways this throw can be done.

How to Throw Knives

Point Forward Throw

The most familiar grip is shown in illustration. The knife is held flat in the hand with the thumb overlapping it. Using an overhand motion, the arm is brought forward, releasing the knife at an angle of about forty-five degrees. You will remember that in most other throws the knife is released parallel to the ground. The angle of release is altered slightly according to the distance. You will have to experiment with your own type of throw for accuracy. The motion of the arm is not circular but straight forward something like that used by an athlete throwing a shot. It is a pushing motion rather than a throwing motion.

It will be obvious when you practice this throw that it is much harder to control than other methods and it is for that reason that we do not use it for regular target throwing.

Underhand Point Forward Throw

The underhand throw is not as accurate as the overhand throw, but there may be times when you will want to use it. This is especially true if a heavy knife is being used. Grasp the handle of the knife with the point held foremost. With a swinging motion the knife is pushed forward with a slight twist of the fingers which brings the blade of the knife up and towards the target.

Overhand Snap Throw

The snap throw is the throw that most of us are familiar with and the one which we have a tendency to want to use. Here at last is your chance! You have probably grasped a jack or penknife blade in your hand and with a flip of your wrist and fingers, shot it toward the target. Sometimes it stuck and sometimes it didn't. Here we see the use of this method. In practicing this throw, it is well to remember that an ordinary overhand throw is used with the exception that there is more push than throw to it. The flip or snap you give it just as it leaves serves only to have the knife make a one-half turn no matter how near or far the target. The secret you must learn with practice is how to judge the distance so that you give the right snap for the one-half turn the knife must spin on its way to the target. The spin on the knife tends to give you a more accurate throw, but it takes practice to get the proper spin.

How to Throw Knives

Underhand Snap Throw

Picture shows the grip used when making the snap throw underhand. It is essentially the same with the exception that the knife is held a little farther up the blade with the knife against the palm and the fingers.

How to Carry Knives for Quick Use

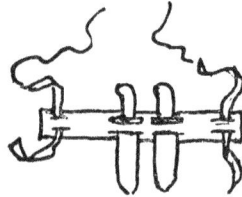

For ordinary use, the regular belt knife sheath is used. This is a convenient place to carry the knife and one that is readily accessible. It is always ready for quick draw in case of emergency, though it is not very well concealed from view. Various types of sheaths are used but the most common one is a regular leather sheath.

While the waist position is as convenient as any, sometimes it is desirable to conceal the view of the knife. This may be done for protective purposes or as part of a stage effect. This may be done in any one of a number of ways. Small knives are sometimes hidden up a loose sleeve with the blade in easy reach to the fingers, but this is a dangerous way to carry a knife for any length of time. Shoulder holsters that are strapped around the chest and shoulder with sheath for one or two knives in front of and below the left shoulder are extremely handy. You reach inside your coat with your right hand as if you were reaching for a pencil in your shirt pocket and pull out a knife. This shoulder harness can be made very easily from leather with either sheath or spring clips to hold knives. It is worn in much the same manner as the shoulder holster for guns.

Illustration 2 shows another popular type of knife holster. This was very popular with Mexican knife throwers. With a somewhat casual movement of the hand, the knife can be whisked out and shot at the target with the popular overhand handle throw described earlier in this chapter. It is also possible to use the end over end handle throw described in an early chapter under "handle grip". Holster can be made for one, two or more knives.

How to Hold Knives for "Close In Fighting"

For hand to hand fighting, the British Commandos and the American Rangers found that the best method of holding the knife was the grip shown in illustration 1. Illustration 2 shows the grip erroneously supposed by most people to be the most protective.

It will be found that if this grip is used it will be harder to guard against and cannot be parried very easily. It has a slashing effect that cuts with more force than the other method.

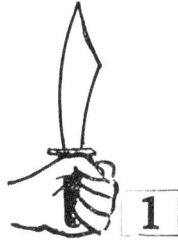 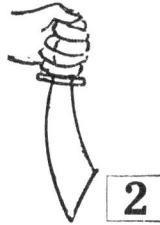

Right   Wrong

A Final Word About Knives

This book has been written primarily for those who want to have some harmless fun throwing knives, but there has been such a demand for more information on stunts, knife fighting, etc., that we have included much information that if not practiced with care can be dangerous. It will be realized at once that the handling of a sharp instrument such as a knife calls for prudence and it is hoped that our readers will exercise a liberal amount of it.

Finally, the instructions given in this book can be applied to almost any type of knife from the Arkansas toothpick (the bowie knife) to the man-and-wife knife (folding pocket or jack knife). Be careful and good luck!

THE ART OF
KNIFE THROWING

BY FRANK DEAN

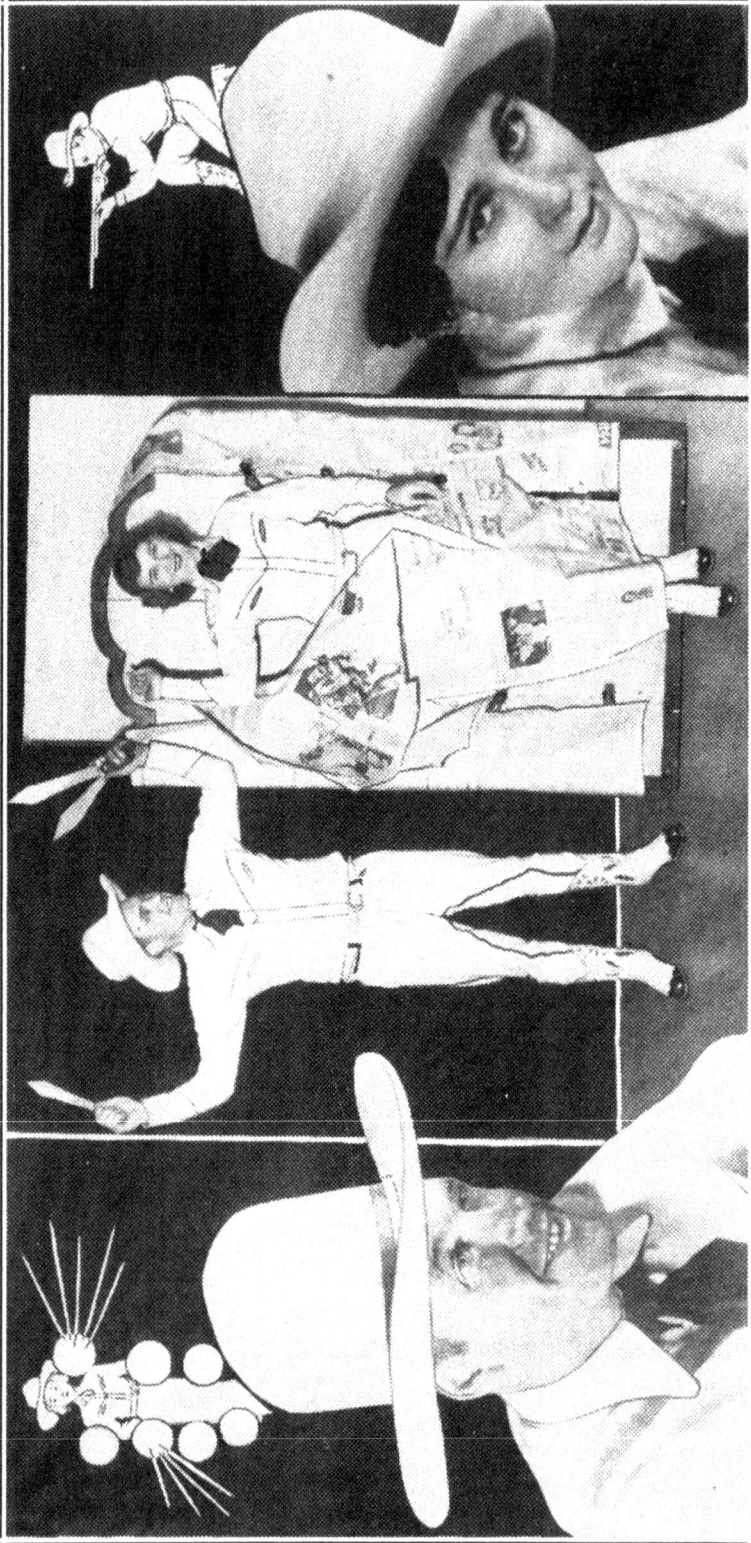

FRANK AND BERNICE DEAN PRESENTING THEIR KNIFE THROWING STUNT, AS DESCRIBED ON PAGE 11.

FOREWORD

●

FRANK DEAN was born in California, and after completing his high school education toured the country with various Circuses, Wild West Shows, and Vaudeville Units.

During the 1929 season with Al. G. Barnes he did his knife throwing act and in addition trick riding and fancy roping numbers. Here he worked with two other noted knife throwers, Frank Chicarello and Bennie Pete.

In 1935 his novelty knife throwing was a sensational feature of the entertainment program presented at the Grand Yokohama Exposition in Japan.

Upon his return in 1935 he started the manufacture of throwing knives. This came about owing to the many requests for knives from people witnessing his act. His 10 inch knife gained popularity and continued requests for information on knife throwing prompted the writing of this book.

This book, written by an actual professional knife thrower, experienced both in the throwing and manufacturing of them, offers much to both beginner and expert in its complete coverage of the subject.

Gathering the material called for an exhaustive search extending over a period of years. The fact that knife throwing has never been popular to any extent with any particular tribe or race has lead to the gleaning of the greater part of the following information from well known knife throwing entertainers and from experiments conducted by the author.

His experience as a soldier in World War II added to his knowledge of the use of the knife in combat.

The few previous works on this art have been very elementary in nature but in compiling this text, every effort has been made to make it complete. To this end a number of original efforts are described and fully explained.

The author will answer all inquiries on individual knife throwing problems if a stamped and self addressed envelope is sent with each request. Frank Dean, San Jose, California.

THE ART OF KNIFE THROWING
BY FRANK DEAN

TO EXPLAIN the origin of knife throwing would be in a great part mere guess work, tho no doubt the first people of this earth caused its inception when they shaped and sharpened their throwing stones into crude knives. Then the projectile arms, such as the bow and arrow, catapults, guns, etc., caused throwing to be of much less value, but even today the throwing of weapons is practised to some extent in various parts of the world. South Sea islanders have their throwing clubs, the Australian Aborigines the boomerang, the Eskimos their harpoons, South African natives their assegais, and the much fictionized knife throwers of both the civilized and savage people, their knives.

Tho an uncommon happening, we know that knives, bolos and machetes have been thrown successfully in the killing of game by natives in various parts of the world, but incidents of their being thrown with deadly effect upon human beings are as scarce as the proverbial hen's teeth.

The idea that a throwing knife is valuable as a weapon for self defense or offense, is erroneous, for it is only practical as entertainment.

True, a great many knives are carried as weapons, some by those skilled in the art of throwing them, but rarely, if ever, are they so used.

The knife fighter would be without a weapon if he threw his knife!

A SWELL HOBBY

AS A SPORT or pastime, many hours of pleasure can be derived from this fascinating science, and its low cost, both initial outlay and upkeep, plus the fact that it requires but little space for practice are advantages making it a very desirable hobby.

You will find that it is not strenuous but a good, mild muscular exercise and in addition, a wonderful training for the eyes.

To begin this pastime, it is necessary to secure a good practice knife, and the fundamental requirement in its construction is sturdiness, for it must be built to withstand hard and rough usage. For this reason the kind of knives available at hardware and sporting goods stores are of little value. Butcher knives as a whole, vibrate and quiver when thrown into a target, and this tendency causes crystalization of the steel which soon results in a broken blade. Hunting knives having a thicker and heavier blade are not apt to break in this manner though their common fault is in the construction of the handles which are seldom made to withstand the rough treatment resulting from their being thrown.

There are knives available for just this purpose and the purchase of these will be found advisable and of small expense.

If you care to construct your own blades they can be easily cut or chiseled out of No. 12 or 14 guage sheet iron and then filed smooth.

If you intend to have your knives nickel plated no doubt you will find it cheaper to use "auto body" steel as it has no scale to be taken off before applying the plating.

Knives made of these soft metals will last indefinitely and tho they may bend they can be easily straightened with little fear of their breaking.

The handles for throwing knives should not be made of wood or any other substance liable to break.

Thick pieces of sole leather or composition rubber as used in shoe soles make handles that last well. These should be attached to the knife with solid rivets 1/8" or more in diameter. The edges of the handles can be rounded up with a file or on an emery wheel.

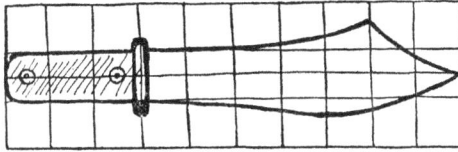

The shape of the knife matters but little; it is the length and the throwing method that count but nevertheless here are three suggested styles. (see illustration No. 1)

(Illustration No. 1)

10 INCH — 3-IN-ONE PATTERN

Using only the top half of the pattern and making both sides of the knife the same will give you a diamond pointed blade. Using the other half of the pattern for both sides of a knife will result in a blade of the sticking knife type.

TARGETS

FOR A TARGET to practice on it is possible to use large cardboard boxes filled with sawdust, a bale of hay or straw or a few boards nailed together.

For a more permanent job it is possible to construct a target of straw similar to those used in archery practice or of wood as used by professional knife throwers in their exhibitions. The most popular variety of lumber used in these is No. 1 quality soft grain sugar pine, but owing to its expense it would probably be passed up by the beginners in favor of a cheaper article. Poplar makes a fair substitute more reasonable in price but slightly harder in grain. Cypress also makes a good soft target. These woods are all more or less spongy and when the knives are removed the hole tends to close slightly and seldom chips. Lumber that chips easily will soon wear out.

A great many knife throwers soak their boards with water to soften them. This is easily done by covering the face of the boards with wet sacks and repeatedly wetting them. In a few hours the wood will soak up enough moisture to keep it soft for a day or two. When throwing into a wet board the knife points should be wiped off after each throw.

The boards thrown at should be at least two inches in thickness for the knives would soon penetrate any lighter material. It should be remembered that the penetration of a knife does not depend entirely upon the keenness of its blade but is governed more by its weight and by the force with which it is thrown.

If two targets are made and the knives thrown from one to the other a great many steps will be saved. This is especially true if the thrower has only a few knives with which to practice.

SPOT TARGETS

SOME PERFORMERS throw at spots or "Bull's Eyes", painted on the backstops usually when demonstrating trick throws. Occasionally the spot targets are small and of the swinging or pendulum type made of two inch soft pine approximately one foot square having a rope or wooden arm by which it is swung from the assistant's hand. Bennie Pete, a California artist, is very adept at this, being able to stick his knife in the "Bull's Eye" every time from a distance of twelve feet. Another effect is to strap the small target over the assistant's chest.

In a recent short subject for M. G. M. the author and Jack Cavanaugh were called upon to do a number of very unusual stunts.

The script called for a "duel" between the knife throwers and each was equipped with a wooden shield target into which his adversary's blades were to stick. During the filming of this a girl had to dance back and forth between the combatants with the knives just missing her head!

KNIFE THROWING ENTERTAINERS

THE KNIVES used by performers always turn end over end in flight and are designed solely for entertainment.

(Illustration No. 2)

(Illustration No. 3)

They vary in length, shape and weight and partly on this account and the difference in individual throwing habits, there is no **standard** measured distance from which the knives are thrown. This is true even tho the majority of professional knife throwers in their exhibitions use a distance of three end for end turns of the knife!

There are two methods of throwing used by these "Impalement Artists" as they are called. One is by the handle as a knife is ordinarily held, the other, by the point of the blades being gripped between the thumb and closed forefinger. The blade should be held in a position parallel with the forearm when grasped in either manner. (see illustration No. 2 and No. 3)

To throw the knife, assume a position, say about five feet away from the target and throw the knife overhand as you would a baseball, observing just how many times it turns end for end after leaving your hand.

Do not try to impart a spinning motion with the wrist, for the throwing action should come thru the shoulder and elbow.

The reason for counting the number of times the knife turns is to ascertain the least possible distance you can stand from the object at which you are throwing.

(Illustration No. 4)

If you are holding the knife by the handle, your least distance will be two end for end turns and when thrown by the blade it will be one end for end turn. By a few experimental throws you will find the proper distance for this result.

If when holding the knife by the handle, it turns end for end twice and sticks in your target from a distance of five feet, this distance minus the length of your arm

By adding the length of your arm to the different turns given on the following chart you arrive at the correct throwing distance for each.

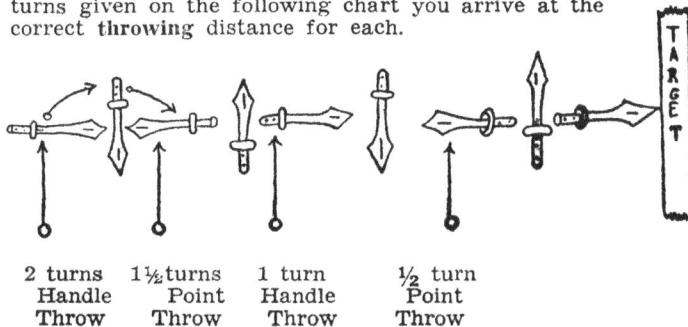

| 2 turns Handle Throw | 1½ turns Point Throw | 1 turn Handle Throw | ½ turn Point Throw |

which we will say is twenty-four inches leaves three feet as the distance necessary for two turns, or one complete revolution of the blade.

By this you can now figure all the distances from which you can successfully stick the knife, for your first distance as you know, would be five feet, the next would be five feet plus the three feet necessary for two more end for end turns and by adding this distance every time you would get eight, eleven and fourteen feet as your new distances.

Now all you have to do is substitute your distances for mine and start practicing. Don't expect perfect results immediately, for it takes considerable practice to learn to throw and continually release the knife in the same manner every time.

When throwing the knife by the point, the distance will be one end for end turn or half a revolution, one and a half revolutions, two and a half revolutions and so on. Never let the blade pivot between the fingers when it is being held by the point, for this error, more or less common with beginners, causes great inaccuracy in throwing, making it extremely difficult to control and maintain the revolutions of the knife.

When removing the knives from the target, it is advisable that you remember to start with the upper ones, for if those lower are pulled out first there is a possibility of receiving a nasty bump on the head from the remaining knives as you raise to remove them.

Regardless of the method you start to learn, remember these DON'TS:

(1) Don't throw with all your might. That's just hard on the knives, the target and you.

(2) Don't practice for too long a period. Try to quit before you are tired and you will find your interest never lagging.

(3) Don't try to increase your throwing distance until the shorter ones are thoroughly mastered.

(4) Don't be in a hurry. Take your time and watch the results of every attempt until you **learn to release the knife in the very same manner every time.**

(5) Don't expect to learn it all the first time you try, for

it's a man's game and requires lots of effort to reach proficiency.

After starting this pastime the devotee would find all the various described methods of holding and throwing the knife of interest and no doubt would soon be experimenting with his own original ideas.

A fine idea for sport with just one knife is to fasten a cord, braided of four strands of twenty-five pounds test linen fishing line to a ring in the handle. The cord should be approximately sixteen feet long and terminate in a small fishing swivel which in turn is secured to the knife.

With this arrangement it is possible to stick your blade in many out-of-the-way places and very easily retrieve it. The danger of losing the knife when wandering about outdoors and throwing at various objects is then minimized to a large extent.

Lizards, as they scampered over or sunned themselves on the bark of oak trees near the author's home, were very often the unwilling targets at which he tested his skill with the flying blade. With the aid of this sixteen foot cord it was an easy matter to remove the knife when it became imbedded in the tree even tho it was ten feet or more overhead.

To accomplish this throw, coil the cord in your left hand in the very same manner a cowboy would his rope, then leave enough slack in the cord between the hand so as not to hamper the movement of your arm. Bring your right arm well back, the knife point being gripped between the thumb and closed forefinger, and then throw it as you would a stone at the same time letting the coils slip through the hand. To retrieve and loosen the knife it is only necessary to jerk the cord back and forth in a long arc a few times.

SPECIAL STUNTS AND TRICK THROWS

WHEN YOU master the simpler methods of throwing, perhaps you will want to go on and learn the more difficult stunts as presented by knife throwers who thrill their audiences with displays of skill in handling the glittering blades.

A good stunt requiring lots of judgment of distance is to cross two knives. There are two ways of doing this. The first is to stand a little closer than the regular distance to the target and throw one knife. You will note then that the knife sticks with the handle pointed downward instead of being at right angles to the target, as is usually the case. Now you must move back past your regular throwing distance as much as you previously moved forward. If you throw the second knife so that the point sticks a few inches directly below the first, it will form a cross when viewed from the side.

The second way is to form a cross visible from the front of the target and to accomplish this the knives must be thrown in from the sides of the target. That is, one knife must be thrown from the extreme left of the target and the other from the extreme right. Both knives should be thrown while standing a little closer than the regular throwing distance in order to have the handles pointing downward as the knives are crossed.

The throwing of more than one knife at a time, using both hands or from one hand will prove an interesting variation.

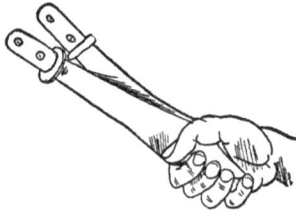

(Illustration No. 6)

The throwing of two or more knives from the same hand simultaneously is not much more difficult than the handling of one knife although the knack of being able to govern their spread calls for considerable practice. The number of blades a person is able to throw in this manner is limited only by the size of the knives and the hand holding them. Most exhibitors prefer two knives for this on account of their ease of handling insuring greater accuracy. Both the point and handle throws are used in this stunt (see illustration No. 6)

BACKWARD THROWS

TO THROW the knives overhand while lying on your back it is only necessary to have the point of the shoulder at the spot the feet are when throwing from a

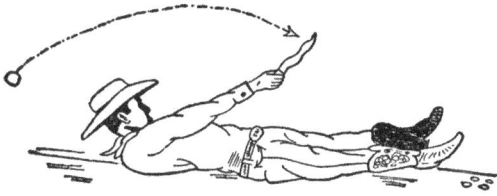

(Illustration No. 7)

standing position. (see ill. No. 7)

There are a number of interesting ways of throwing the knives while standing with your back to the target.

Looking backwards under your throwing arm as you throw your blades into the backstop is quite easily accomplished if the thrower stands at the same distance he ordinarily throws from. (See illustration No. 8)

To make this throw while looking backwards over the opposite shoulder makes an interesting and amusing experiment. Upon the first attempt the thrower will usually miss the target by a long way.

(Illustration No. 8)

Throwing the knives from between the legs calls for a few experimental throws in order to find the correct throwing distance. (See illustration No. 9)

(Illustration No. 9)

(Illustration No. 10)

THE LIFTED LEG THROW

THIS STUNT is, I believe, only demonstrated by one professional and is performed as the thrower is walking from left to right (if he is right handed) and parallel with the target. Walking slowly, the knives are thrown from beneath each leg as it is lifted for the forward steps. (See illustration No. 10) Here the under hand method of throwing is necessary and it will be found to require a great deal of practice in order to gain any marked degree of accuracy with this unusual throw.

Bennie Pete, formerly of the Al G. Barnes and the Tom Mix Circus and other shows is the originator, I believe, of this particular method of throwing.

STUNTS USED IN A KNIFE THROWING ACT

THE VARIOUS routines of knife stunts as used in show business all have individuality and reflect the performer's own ideas of showmanship. (See illustration No. 11)

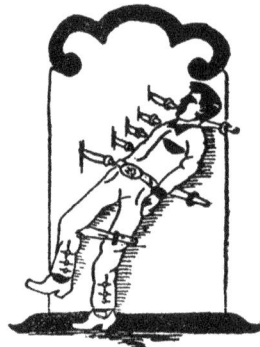

Most of the following stunts could be done in various ways such as throwing knives from a prone position or throwing two or more knives at one time or perhaps throwing the knives out from within a rope spun around the body as a California cowboy does. These ideas will probably suggest others to you and help you conceive

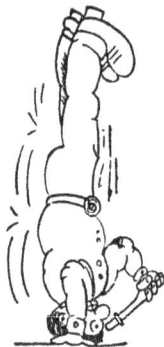

(Illustration No. 11)   (Illustration No. 12)

your own routine.

The common routines of knife stunts as performed on the stage and in the circus usually consist of but two or three positions of impalement and perhaps a string, paper or flower cutting trick.

The most popular position of the assistant is standing close to the knife board squarely facing the thrower with the arms hanging at the sides. Sometimes the assistant

Note Capt. Allen's slightly blurred knife hitting just above his assistant's head.

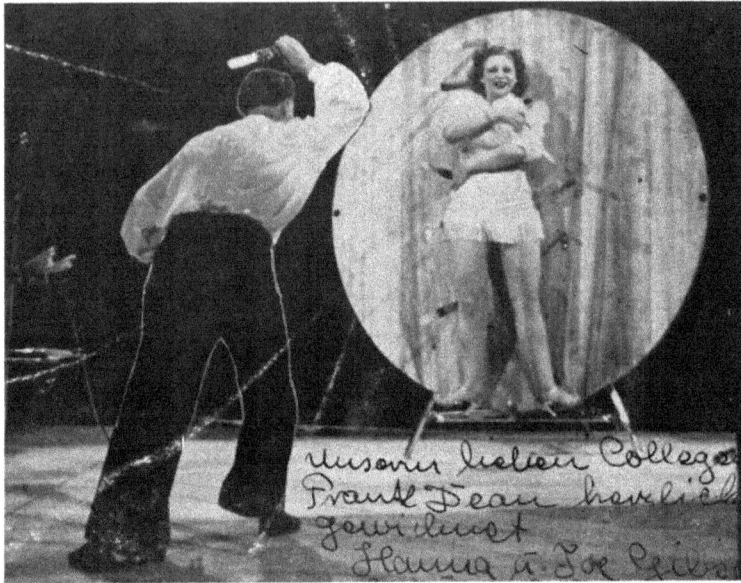

The Gibsons, presenting their sensational knife throwing act. The board used is round and mounted on an axel like a wheel. His assistant spins rapidly as she is firmly held on the revolving target whlie Otto Gibson throws his gleaming blade around her

For his finale, a paper hoop cover is placed over his assistant. She is outlined with knives again while under this paper, as the solid wood wheel is rapidly revolved. The only part of the assistant showing from beneath the paper hoop is her feet. All the knife thrower's timing must be gauged fro mthese protruding shoes.

Tex Orton, famous circus knife thrower outlining his assistant as described on page 12.

Blindfolded, with a hood over his head, Tex Orton presents this thrilling stunt.

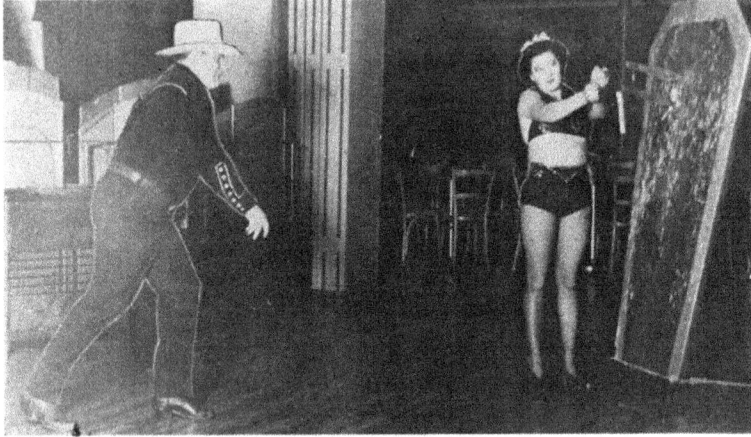

The paper cutting as described on page 13. Tex Orton demonstrating.

stands sideways but in either way the knives are thrown close to the body and stuck in a vertical row.

Another way is to throw three knives into the board in such a way that the assistant walks in and assumes a back bending position, one knife against the small of the back, another beneath the back of the neck and the third lower so that one leg can be placed over it; the knife then being beneath the knee. After the assistant assumes this position the remainder of the knives are thrown outlining the body. (See illustration No. 12)

Circling the assistant with knives as he is seated upon a chair or outlining the profile of the throat and head with knives thrown closely together or outlining the entire body are other popular stunts. In the latter trick the assistant stands with the arms outstretched against the knife board and the feet braced widely apart allowing plenty of room for the blades. This stunt properly done requires thirty or more knives.

Another great impalement feature is the "penning in" of the assistant and to accomplish this the performer throws from two positions, one from the extreme right of the target and one to the extreme left. With long knives, say about 16 or 18 inches in length, it is possible in this way to stick them close enough to make it hard for the assistant to squeeze out from between the two lines of knives.

OUTLINING AN ASSISTANT YOU CAN'T SEE

THE SPECTACULAR stunt of throwing knives around the assistant after he has been completely hidden by a newspaper covering is the masterpiece of knife throwers. To accomplish this, which you will want to do after you have mastered the other impalement tricks, is much simpler than it appears to be, tho of course, dangerous to an extreme. A number of times I have seen assistants receive deep wounds as a result of this presentation, but if everything is figured carefully and if the assistant is given the proper instructions before attempting the trick the danger of an accident is minimized.

In the first place newspaper or some other paper material must be pasted together to form a large covering that can be placed over the assistant and thumbtacked to the back of the board.

If this is done, the only part of the assistant visible would be the feet and **they** provide the information that the knife thrower must have.

The knives are lined up, starting from the bottom about six inches away from each foot.

The assistant must know the side you start throwing the knives on and how many are to be thrown there **before** you start on the other side. **He must know this,** to shift his weight from one foot to the other in order to give the the maximum amount of space. That is if you are throwing on your assistant's **left** he shifts his weight to his **right** foot bending his knee slightly and in doing so moves the upper part of his body at least six inches farther away from the knives as they are lined up vertically a few inches away from the feet. After throwing the number of knives agreed upon on the first side, the assistant shifts his weight to the opposite foot and the remainder of the knives are thrown. As the last knife is thrown, the assistant steps out, breaking the paper and takes a bow.

The shifting of the body beneath the paper is not noticeable to the audience when well rehearsed and adds a great deal of safety to this wonderful stunt.

Another way of doing this trick is to judge the distance from the side of the knife board and throw the knives accordingly.But using the position of the feet as a guide provides the surest method of estimating the proper distance.

A good thing to remember when doing impalement stunts of any sort is to begin sticking the knives near the legs or arms and gradually working up as you near the more vital points, the throat and head. In this way you know exactly how much variation there is in your throws and can work closer with safety.

To vary this routine considerably, a different shape knife could be used for each different effect. (See illustration No. 13) A knife thrower now touring the country

with a carnival side show varies his routine by using twelve inch nails or spikes.

Steve Clemento, a well known impalement artist of Hollywood who has thrown at more moving picture stars than any other man has been called upon to do this with nearly every form of edged weapon. To show his complete mastery of the art he skillfully throws pick axes,

(Illus. No. 13)

tomahawks and even the top of a stove in his regular act!

An unusual impalement stunt is to fasten small toy balloons to various parts of the assistant's body, then as he stands with his back against the board the knives are thrown breaking the balloons and sticking into the wood.

PAPER CUTTING

A PAPER CUTTING trick easily done is accomplished with the aid of a specially prepared piece of folded paper. In making this practically any kind of paper can be used tho a piece out of the classified ad section of a newspaper is ideal, for reasons I will explain later.

Cut out a piece about 5 inches wide and one foot long, and then fold it lengthwise until it is approximately one inch wide. The loose side should be pasted or glued down and when dry the piece should be cut into two parts. Now by neatly telescoping one piece into the other for a short distance, you have your trick paper ready for action. The joint is not noticeable more than a few feet away, mainly on account of the even printing of the newspaper.

Now, when the end of this prepared paper is held in the hand or mouth of the assistant, it is only necessary to **hit** the paper with the knife in order to produce a realistic cutting stunt.

The paper should be held away from the target into which the knife sticks the distance of **one half of an end for end turn of the knife.**

CUTTING FLOWERS

T HIS PRESENTATION is marvelous in appearance and is not faked, as was the preceding paper cutting trick. Three or four flowers can even be cut at once! On cutting them it must be remembered to have them held just **one half turn** of the knife away from the target. This distance is where the knife is in a **vertical positon** as it turns through the air. **The full length of the blade then is in position to cut flowers.**

You can use a dull knife on most flowers, as the force and speed of the turns of the knife and the brittleness of the stems make this possible.

The flowers should be fresh for best results, and the following ten kinds have been listed on account of their being especially suitable for this stunt.

DANDELIONS   GERANIUMS   DAHLIAS   MARIGOLDS   TULIPS
CHINA LILIES   NARCISSUS   DAISIES   POPPIES   IRIS

Nearly any hollow, watery stem flower is ideal, as they are severed at the place they are struck by the knife. Others having harder and tougher stems are not so easily cut and usually then only the flower or bud is clipped off.

Roses and carnations are representative of this latter group.

STRING CUTTING

HERE IS A STUNT that seems to take the utmost skill in its accomplishment. But, the truth is, it is as simple as the preceding trick.

The assistant has a piece of string that he holds, one end wrapped around each hand, the same distance away from the knife board that the flowers and paper were held. If the hands are held about 12 or 14 inches apart, holding the string taut at one side of the body and parallel with the wasteline, it is an easy matter then for the performer to throw his knife and cut the string. (See illustration No. 14).

Another way of presenting this string cutting effect is to have the assistant stoop or kneel in front of the board, holding the taut string just above his head (See illustration No. 15) In this demonstration it is a good idea to cut the string slightly to one side of the head of the assistant, and not directly above it. This obviously makes it safer, for the variation in knife throwing is greater vertically than horizontally.

CUTTING A MOVING STRING

If two people hold the ends of a string and rapidly move it up and down, it can be easily severed with a

(Illustration No. 14)   (Illustration No. 15)

thrown knife. The important thing being to have the hold-ers instructed **not to move the string up and down more than the length of the blade of the knife.** This string cut-ting stunt is done like the other cutting stunts with the cord being held away from the backstop at a distance equal to one half of one end for end turn of the knife.

Blue or black heavy cotton yarn is very effective in presenting the tricks mentioned above, for it shows up well and is easily severed.

HALVING A SWINGING APPLE

TO CUT AN APPLE, a potato, or some like object, while it is moving in the form of a pendulum suspend-ed by a wire in front of a knife board, is a trick well worth adding to a routine.

The support for the pendulum is a piece of wood fast-ened at right angles to the knife board and extending out the distance of **half of an end for end turn** of the knife. In the end of this support there must be a nail, or screw head protruding, on which the wire can be looped. This wire should be of steel, about 30 inches in length, and may be an E string from a guitar. The wire must have a good loop made in each end, one formed like a noose to hold the apple, and the other to loop over the nail.

When the noose is placed over the apple, it should be pulled tight enough to cut thru the outer skin a short dis-tance. This prevents the apple from slipping out of the loop and also leaves that much less to cut.

The apple is started swinging, and as it goes past the

center and starts upward, the knife is thrown above the wire, striking midway of the swing. Now, if this is timed properly, the blade of the knife hits the wire and slides or glances down and cuts the apple! A little practice will enable you to judge just the right time and place to throw.

This can also be done as the assistant swings the apple back and forth as he holds the wire in his hand.

THE "WILLIAM TELL" APPLE STUNT

S PLITTING AN apple with a thrown knife as it rests upon an assistant's head is accomplished from a distance of one end for end turn of the blade. To improve the looks of this short throw the performer stands away from the target far enough to enable him to take one step and lean forward to the correct throwing distance. After the throw he steps back to his starting position. The step forward, the throw, and the step backward must all be done quickly and smoothly to create the illusion of greater distance.

When making the throw the knife is whipped forward sideways. That is, the blade **tumbles end for end horizontally and not vertically** as is usually the case.

As a safeguard a light steel lining can be placed in the hat upon which the apple rests.

This sensational stunt was performed for years by one of the country's best known knife throwers and was often a newsreel subject.

FIRE KNIVES

I MPALEMENT ACTS using fire knives are seldom seen, on account of various difficulties arising mainly from the locations chosen for their presentation. Indoors, fire insurance regulations prohibit them, and outdoors a slight breeze would make it quite uncomfortable for the assistant standing in the flaming circle.

The knives used have special handles which are dipped in kerosene or other volatile oil, and on this account, are thrown only by the point grip.

There are various other ways in which this impalement stunt can be demonstrated, a novel one being to stick the knives unlighted and close together on both sides of the assistant, keeping **two burning** knives for the last, and throwing one on each side directly below the lowest one there. These knives cause all the others to catch fire, forming an instantaneous pillar of flame on each side of the assistant.

A damp cloth can be wrapped around the handles to extinguish the fire as the knives are removed from the board.

AXE, CLEAVER AND TOMAHAWK THROWING

I N THROWING a tomahawk, camp axe, battle axe or cleaver, two methods of holding them are used. When thrown into the backstop by one method, the weapon

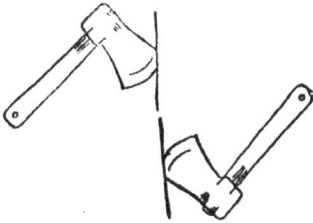

sticks with the handle pointed up; the other down. (See illustrations No. 16 and No. 17.)

With a common camp axe having a twelve inch handle, try throwing from a distance of five ordinary walking steps away from the target. From this point the

(Illustrations 16 and 17)

axe should stick with the handle pointed down, if it is held when thrown with the blunt, or hammer side up.

To throw from about seven or seven and a half steps, turn the axe over to bring the sharp edge up. This causes the axe to become imbedded in the target with the handle pointed up.

Cleavers, Tomahawks and battle axes (See illustrations No. 18 and No. 19) can be thrown the same way. The throwing distance depends mostly upon the length of the handle. A short handled axe, when thrown, turns over more times than a long handled one if they are both thrown from the same distance.

To throw heavy axes having a handle of about 36 inches, hold them head down with the sharp edge toward the target and throw with an

(No. 20)

(No. 18)

(No. 19)

underhand swing. (See number 20.) From a distance of about twelve steps, the axe should make one complete revolution and stick in the target with the handle pointed up.

KNIFE FIGHTING

F ICTION HAS popularized the deadly knife thrower who unerringly severs the jugular vein of his victim with his flying blade. Very few people, if any, have ever witnessed such an event. An eye witness to this sort of happening is yet to be found.

Natives in the Philippines and in Mexico, tho, have been known to clip off the heads, or impale small game from fifteen to no more than twenty feet.

To be really effective in fast, close fighting, a knife would have to travel point foremost at all times. This difficult and rarely seen throw differs from the system used by professional entertainers, for their knives turn end over end when thrown, and are only stuck from certain predetermined distances.

In attempting to learn a "point foremost" throw, the tyro must remember that the design and balance alone of even a specially made knife will not cause it to go thru the air like a spear. Even an arrow cannot be grasped by the feathered end, thrown like a dart, and be expected to remain with the shaft always parallel with the line of flight.

There are numerous ways of executing this throw properly, but the two following methods are the most used.

The more accurate of the two is the "Overhand" throw, in which the knife is held with the butt of the handle resting upon the palm as the thumb presses the hilt against the open fingers. (See illustration No. 21) With a direct overhand motion, the arm is brought forward, releasing the knife, not parallel with the forearm, but at an angle of about forty-five degrees. This angle of release changes slightly as the throwing distance is varied, and is also affected by the amount of "push" used.

(Illustration No. 21)

When throwing, it is well to remember to keep the knife as straight in line with the target as possible. From the beginning of the throw to the moment of releasing the knife, the arm should not describe a circular motion, but should be brought straight forward. The whole secret, then, is that this weapon should be **pushed** more than thrown, in somewhat the same manner an athlete would use in handling the sixteen pound shot.

To throw the knife by the second or "Underhand" method, grasp the handle in the closed fingers, with the point held foremost, the thumb resting against the blade, and impart a spinning motion as the knife is released.

This is done in very near the same manner as one would roll a cigaret or pencil in the fingers.

With either of these two methods the best results will be had at distances less than twenty feet, although it is possible, with practice, to control the knife with a fair degree of accuracy over much greater distances.

A far more common trick, a favorite of the Mexican knife thrower, is the

Illustration No. 22 "end for end" throw, in which the knife turns over but once, regarless of any variation in the distances thrown from.

To do this, the knife is grasped by the point and thrown "overhand". The wrist controls the angle of the release of the knife, and this must be supplemented, over longer distances, by various amounts of "push" as explained in the earlier paragraph. (See illustration No. 22)

To make this throw by the seldom used "underhand" method, the knife is held with the point of the blade near the wrist, the thumb resting midway between the handle and the tip, holding the knife (Illustration No. 23) against the palm and fingers of the open hand. (See illustration No. 23)

This method of holding the knife can also be used in making the "overhand" throw and is found by some to

(Illustration No. 24)   (Illustration No. 25)

be an easier delivery.

In both the underhand and the overhand throws, the thrower governs the angle of releasing the knife by his mental estimate of the distance to be thrown. This obviously can only be done thru practice.

If you have a fine expensive knife that you want to learn to throw, it is best to secure a **practice** throwing knife of the same length and style. If you don't at least practice your throws on a bale of hay or straw, and try to give your knife as little abuse as possible. Never throw a sharp edged knife that you want to remain that way, at the wire wrapped sides of a bale.

When carrying the knife ready for a quick draw, a number of methods are used. The most common being to carry it at the belt. Moros and other natives carry their knives at their waist in wooden sheaths made of two pieces of hard wood that are held together by a fibre string. In an emergency, by just jerking the knife forward, the string is cut and the blade released.

In Japan at one time the warriors carried small throwing knives (Ko-Zukas) in the sheath of the Dai-To and Naga-Wakizashi swords.

Of course, some knives are carried where they can not be seen and of these methods the most popular place of concealment is at the back of the neck. (See illustration No. 24 and illustration No. 25) One or more knives can be easily hidden in this manner. Short knives are sometimes hidden up a loose shirt sleeve with the handle within easy reach of the other hand.

Boot tops and shoulder holster type sheaths are also to be found. The shoulder harness referred to had spring clips for two knives.

Now if you have practised all the stunts previously described and really kept up your interest in the hobby you will no doubt want to make one of these holdouts and try your skill at the quick draw.

With the back of the outfit as illustrated in figure 24 you can grasp the end of your knife handle and make a fast, smooth throw using either the "no turn" throw (see page 18) or the two revolution handle throw. (see page 5)

With the shirt sleeve holdout in which the sheath is fastened to the left forearm the knife handle is just above the end of the cuff and is easily grasped in the right hand as the hands are brought together.

(Illustration No. 26)
The knife grip as fiction has it and . . .

(Illustration No. 27)
As it actually is held in hand-to-hand fighting.

It is not advisable to try to fasten your knife to your arm so that you only need to jerk your arm forward to release it. As it falls down into your hand you may very easily be cut if you use a sharp edged blade. This stunt is all right in fiction but not in practice.

Another thing seldom pictured or described correctly is the proper manner of holding a knife in a fight. It is not held as pictured in illustration No. 26, for a downward thrust when the knife is held in this manner could easily be parried.

With the knife held as shown in illustration No. 27 a forward thrust or a cut or slash to right or left gives full benefit of the cutting edge and is a great deal harder for one's opponent to guard against.

NOTES

NOTES

Coachwhip Publications

CoachwhipBooks.com

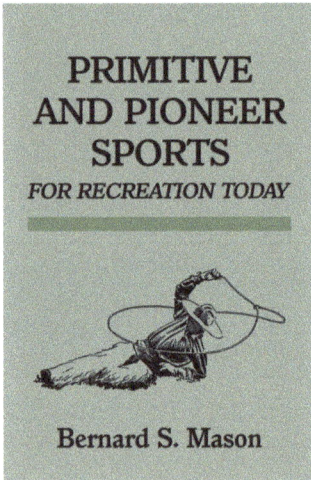

PRIMITIVE AND PIONEER SPORTS
FOR RECREATION TODAY
Bernard S. Mason

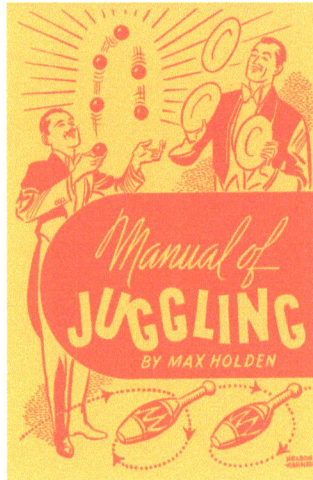

Manual of JUGGLING
BY MAX HOLDEN

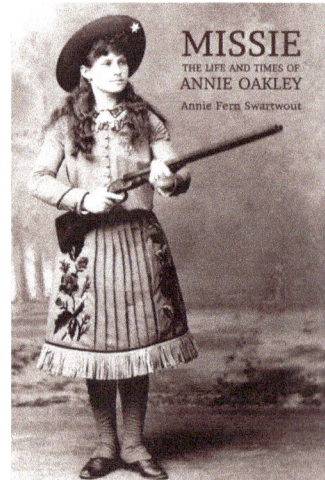

MISSIE
THE LIFE AND TIMES OF ANNIE OAKLEY
Annie Fern Swartwout

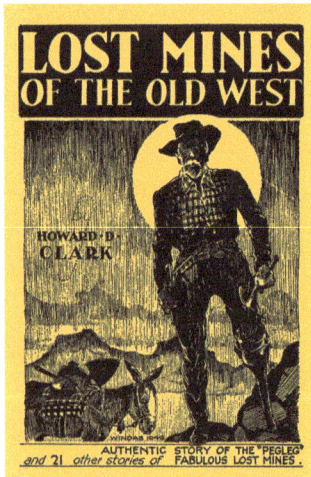

LOST MINES OF THE OLD WEST
By HOWARD D. CLARK
AUTHENTIC STORY OF THE "PEGLEG" and 21 other stories of FABULOUS LOST MINES.

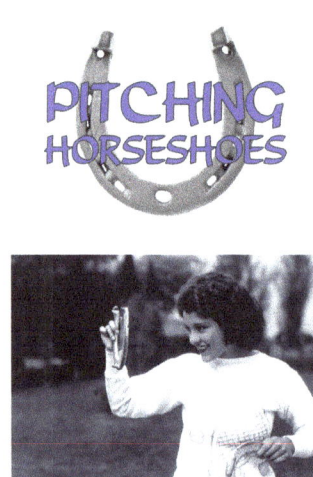

PITCHING HORSESHOES

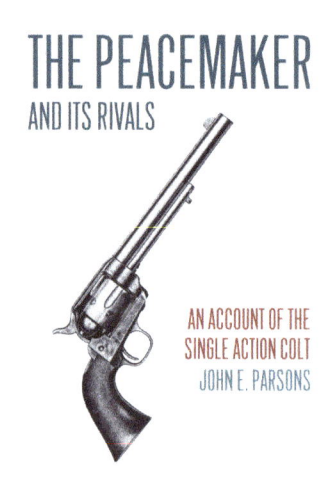

THE PEACEMAKER AND ITS RIVALS
AN ACCOUNT OF THE SINGLE ACTION COLT
JOHN E. PARSONS

COACHWHIP PUBLICATIONS

ALSO AVAILABLE

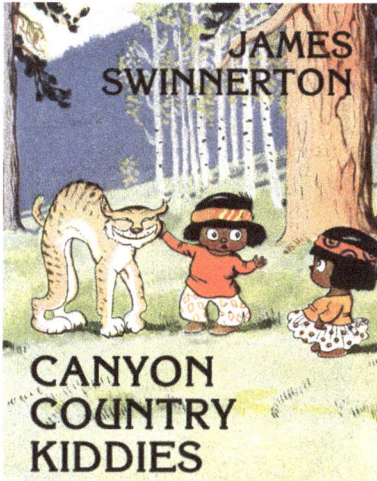

JAMES SWINNERTON

CANYON COUNTRY KIDDIES

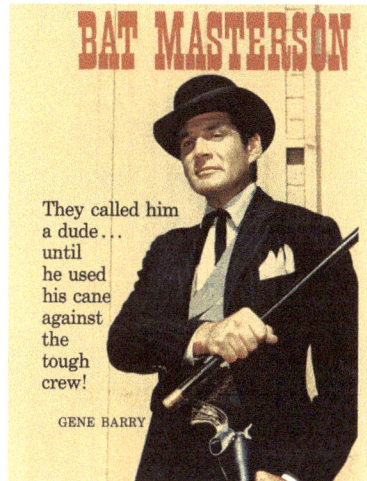

BAT MASTERSON

They called him a dude... until he used his cane against the tough crew!

GENE BARRY

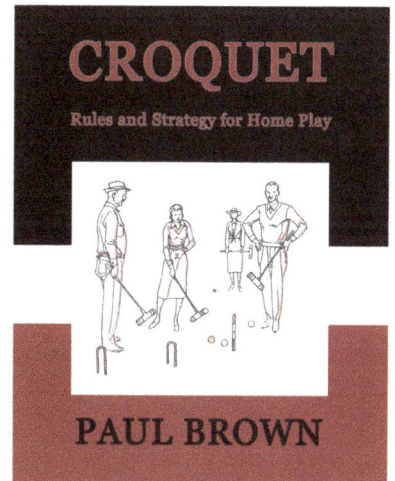

CROQUET

Rules and Strategy for Home Play

PAUL BROWN

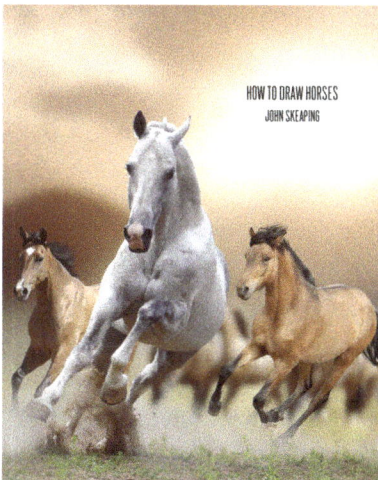

HOW TO DRAW HORSES
JOHN SKEAPING

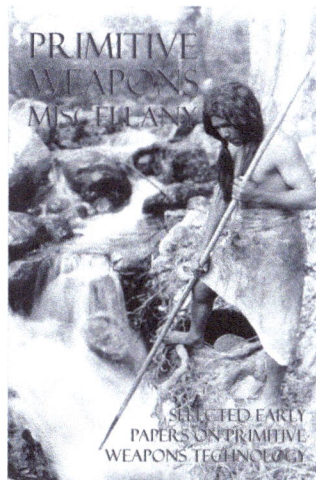

PRIMITIVE WEAPONS MISCELLANY

SELECTED EARLY PAPERS ON PRIMITIVE WEAPONS TECHNOLOGY

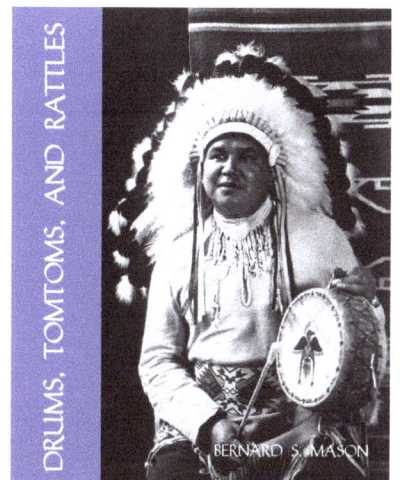

DRUMS, TOMTOMS, AND RATTLES

BERNARD S. MASON